Welcome, Children!
A Child's Mass Book

This book belongs to

Gavin Walsh.

I am a member of the faith community of

Our Lady of Hope parish

in the city of _Middle Village_.

I attend school at _O.L.H.C.A._.

Today's date is _10/19/16_.

Draw or glue a picture of yourself in this box.

Pflaum Publishing Group
Dayton, OH
Milwaukee, WI

A note to parents and catechists
Faith is a wonderful gift to share with the children in your care. This book is a simple and reverent resource for introducing the Eucharist. Children can "make it their own" by solving the puzzles, coloring the pictures, and following along during Mass.

Whether you teach formally or informally, your relationship is the key to nurturing your children's faith. Your loving presence affirms them in the way that God affirms each person. With that joy, they can claim their identity as children of God.

Text and Activities by Jean Buell
First and foremost, Jean is a parent who wants her home to be a place of faith, hope, and love. In addition to parenting and writing, Jean facilitates worship and learning experiences for children and families in her home state of Minnesota. Other titles in this popular series for children include books on the Bible, saints, rosary, sacraments, and making faithful choices. Available from Pflaum Publishing Group.

Cover illustrations by Elizabeth Swisher
Interior design by Jean Buell and Ellen Wright
Edited by Jean Larkin

Nihil obstat: Reverend Monsignor John F. Murphy, *censor librorum*, April 5, 2004

Imprimatur: †Most Reverend Timothy M. Dolan, Archbishop of Milwaukee, April 19, 2004

Published with the approval of the Committee on Divine Worship, United States Conference of Catholic Bishops

Excerpts from the English translation of *The Roman Missal, Third Edition* © 2011, International Commission on English in the Liturgy Corporation. All rights reserved.

© 2011 Pflaum Publishing Group. Published in Milwaukee, WI. All rights reserved. No portion of this text may be reproduced in any way or for any use without the written permission of the publisher.

Fourth Printing December 2014

ISBN 978-1-935042-71-6

Welcome, Children!

You are invited to attend a special gathering. Yes, YOU! This gathering is called the Mass. It is a celebration of friendship with Jesus. Are you ready? Come on in!

Write the name of your church on top of this door. Color the spaces like a checkerboard. Read the words from the first color. Then read the words from the second color.

Welcome, Children!

Welcome to the worship space. This is the large area where Mass takes place. There's plenty of room for you!

Follow the arrows to find your seat in a pew. Begin a new word with each **bold** letter. Write the words in the pews on the left. When you come to the arrow that leads into your pew, write your name. Add your family members and friends in the remaining pews.

The Bible reveals a hidden guest. Look in Matthew 18:20. Write the guest's name. _____

4

Welcome, Children!

The worship space includes many sacred objects. They remind us that Jesus is present. Which ones can you name?

Complete the words and pictures below. Find similar objects in your church. Jesus is present with complete love!

The CROSS carries our hope in Jesus.

CANDLES light the way to Jesus.

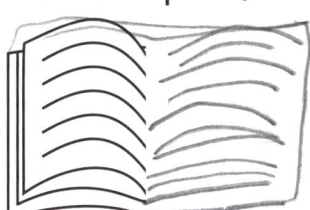

The BIBLE tells Jesus' good news.

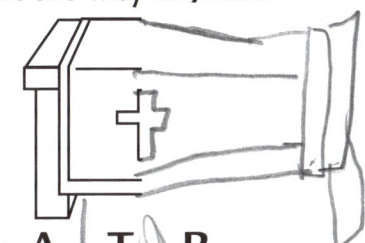

The ALTAR represents the table of Jesus.

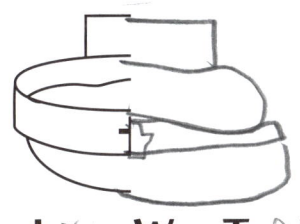

HOLY WATER sprinkles us with new life.

The TABERNACLE holds the Holy Eucharist.

A candle glows near the tabernacle to show that Jesus is present in the Holy Eucharist. To show respect, we genuflect.

Stand    Kneel    Stand

5

Welcome, Children!

Before Mass begins, take some time to pray quietly. Imagine that Jesus is sitting right next to you. In your thoughts, tell him about your week. When did you feel happy? Sad? Angry? Afraid?

After your prayer, look for banners in the worship space. Their colors show the seasons of the Church year. These seasons help us celebrate our friendship with Jesus.

Color the banners below. Fill in the names of the seasons. They are in this order: Advent, Christmas, Lent, Easter, and Ordinary Time. What season is it now?

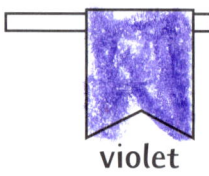
violet

During **Advent**, we wait for Jesus.

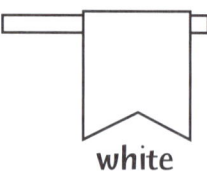
white

During **Christmas**, we celebrate Jesus' birth.

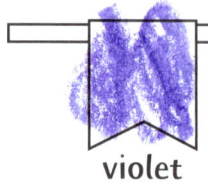
violet

During **Lent**, we renew our promises to Jesus.

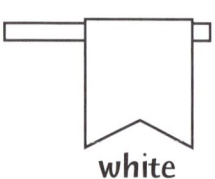
white

During **Easter**, we share new life with Jesus.

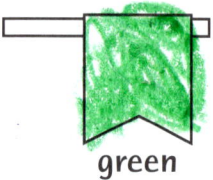
green

During **Ordinary Time**, we learn from Jesus.

INTRODUCTORY RITES

Opening song

Greeting

Priest: In the name of the Father, and of the Son, and of the Holy Spirit.
People: Amen.

Priest: The grace of our Lord Jesus Christ
and the love of God,
and the communion of the Holy Spirit
be with you all.
People: And with your spirit.

*During the **Greeting**, we make the Sign of the Cross. This prayer reminds us that we are baptized.*

In the name of the Father,

and of the Son,

and of the Holy

Spirit.

Amen.

Welcome, Children!

In the **Penitential Act**, we think about the choices we make. Imagine that Jesus is standing right next to you. He loves you, and he forgives you for unloving choices.

Jesus also reminds us how to make loving choices. Follow the code and fill in the blanks. Follow the reminder, too.

L O V E   G O D

W I T H   A L L   Y O U R   H E A R T

H E A R T   A N D   Y O U R   M I N D

A N D   S O U L   .

L O V E   Y O U R

N E I G H B O R   A S

Y O U R S E L F .

From Matthew 22:37-39

Code

⊞ = A	≋ = F	🐑 = L	🐟 = R	✑ = V
📖 = B	🍇 = G	🙏 = M	☆ = S	♀ = W
🕊 = D	✟ = H	✝ = N	⌂ = T	⛪ = Y
🕯 = E	@ = I	♡ = O	☧ = U	

Penitential Act

Priest: Brethren (brothers and sisters), let us acknowledge our sins,
and so prepare ourselves to celebrate the sacred mysteries.

Priest and **People:**

I confess to almighty God
and to you, my brothers and sisters,
that I have greatly sinned,
in my thoughts and in my words,
in what I have done and in what I have failed to do,
through my fault, through my fault,
through my most grievous fault;
therefore I ask blessed Mary ever-Virgin,
all the Angels and Saints,
and you, my brothers and sisters,
to pray for me to the Lord our God.

> As a sign of sorrow for our sins, we "strike our breast," which means we gently tap our hearts three times with our fists.

Priest: May almighty God have mercy on us,
forgive us our sins,
and bring us to everlasting life.
People: Amen.

Kyrie

Priest:	Lord, have mercy.	(or)	Kyrie, eleison.
People:	Lord, have mercy.	(or)	Kyrie, eleison.
Priest:	Christ, have mercy.	(or)	Christe, eleison.
People:	Christ, have mercy.	(or)	Christe, eleison.
Priest:	Lord, have mercy.	(or)	Kyrie, eleison.
People:	Lord, have mercy.	(or)	Kyrie, eleison.

Welcome, Children!

Jesus forgives us and restores our friendship with God. That is why he came! When he was born, the angels sang a song of praise. In the **Gloria**, we praise God, too.

Copy the Gloria's first two lines onto the banner below. Then color the stained-glass window. What story does it tell?

The angels' story is in your Bible. Look in Luke 2:8-14.

Gloria

Priest and **People:**

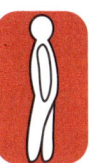

Glory to God in the highest,
and on earth peace to people of good will.
We praise you,
we bless you,
we adore you,
we glorify you,
we give you thanks for your great glory,
Lord God, heavenly King,
O God, almighty Father.
Lord Jesus Christ, Only Begotten Son,
Lord God, Lamb of God, Son of the Father,
you take away the sins of the world,
    have mercy on us;
you take away the sins of the world,
    receive our prayer;
you are seated at the right hand of the Father,
    have mercy on us.
For you alone are the Holy One,
you alone are the Lord,
you alone are the Most High,
Jesus Christ,
with the Holy Spirit,
in the glory of God the Father.
Amen.

Collect Prayer

Priest: Let us pray.

We pray silently while the priest prays aloud.

Priest: For ever and ever.
People: Amen.

Welcome, Children!

When we gather for celebrations, we often tell stories. This part of Mass is called the **Liturgy of the Word**. We read stories from the Bible. Listen carefully—God speaks to our hearts, and Jesus tells us good news!

True or False: A Bible is one book. Start at the arrow, and read every other word. Write the message you discover.

books • A • Bible • many • bound • one • is • really • into

_____

_____

During the **Homily**, we learn about the Bible stories. Listen carefully. How many times do you hear the word love? How many times do you hear the word Jesus? Think of other faith-words and listen for them. Write them in the box on the next page. How many times do you hear them?

LITURGY OF THE WORD

First Reading—*We listen to a reading from the Old Testament, written before Jesus was born.*
Reader: The word of the Lord.
People: Thanks be to God.

Responsorial Psalm—*We join in a prayer called a Psalm. It is read or sung.*

Second Reading—*We listen to a reading from the New Testament, written after Jesus was born.*
Reader: The word of the Lord.
People: Thanks be to God.

Gospel Acclamation—*Alleluia is a word of praise and happiness and it is usually sung. During the seasons of Advent and Lent, instead of Alleluia, we say another short prayer, called an invocation.*
Cantor: Alleluia!
People: Alleluia!

We praise God silently while a short verse is read.
People: Alleluia!

Gospel Reading
Priest or Deacon: The Lord be with you.
People: And with your spirit.
Priest: A reading from the holy Gospel according to [Matthew, Mark, Luke, or John].
People: Glory to you, O Lord.

> With your thumb, make a small sign of the cross on your forehead, your lips, and your heart, and silently pray, "God be in my mind, on my lips, and in my heart."

We listen to the good news that Jesus brings!
Priest or Deacon: The Gospel of the Lord.
People: Praise to you, Lord Jesus Christ.

Homily

Love ___ _____ __ _____ __

Jesus___ _____ __ _____ __

Welcome, Children!

In the **Profession of Faith**, we state our belief in God, Jesus, and the Holy Spirit—the Holy Trinity. This prayer is called the creed. It describes God's power and love.

Look at the puzzle below. The words outside the triangle represent some of the many ways that we experience God's love. Find the same words inside the triangle and circle them.

God

Parent **Creator**

Teacher **Lifegiver**

```
              Y
            D E P
          N G S F A
        E H E L P E R
      I U S G O D M E E
    R P R A Y V B J O Y N
  F A C L I F E G I V E R T
J E S U S H O L Y S P I R I T
Y T E A C H E R N C R E A T O R K
```

Jesus   **Friend**   **Helper**   **Holy Spirit**

How do you experience God's love? Outside the triangle, write your own words to describe God's love.

Profession of Faith (Nicene Creed)

Priest and **People:**

I believe in one God,
   the Father almighty,
   maker of heaven and earth,
   of all things visible and invisible.
I believe in one Lord Jesus Christ,
   the Only Begotten Son of God,
   born of the Father before all ages.
   God from God, Light from Light,
   true God from true God,
   begotten, not made, consubstantial with the Father;
   through him all things were made.
   For us men and for our salvation
   he came down from heaven,
   and by the Holy Spirit was incarnate of the
      Virgin Mary,
   and became man.
For our sake he was crucified under Pontius Pilate,
   he suffered death and was buried,
   and rose again on the third day
   in accordance with the Scriptures.
   He ascended into heaven
   and is seated at the right hand of the Father.
   He will come again in glory to judge
   the living and the dead
   and his kingdom will have no end.
I believe in the Holy Spirit, the Lord, the giver of life,
   who proceeds from the Father and the Son,
   who with the Father and the Son is adored and glorified,
   who has spoken through the prophets.
I believe in one, holy, catholic and apostolic Church.
   I confess one Baptism for the forgiveness of sins
   and I look forward to the resurrection of the dead
   and the life of the world to come. Amen.

Welcome, Children!

St. Patrick used a shamrock to teach about God. A shamrock leaf is one leaf in three parts. The Holy Trinity is one God in three persons—Father, Son, and Holy Spirit.

Make a shamrock with green paper. Teach someone about the Holy Trinity. Tell them about the ways that God loves us.

Sometimes we pray the Apostles' Creed instead of the Nicene Creed.

Profession of Faith (Apostles' Creed)

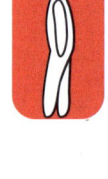

Priest and **People:**

I believe in God,
    the Father almighty,
    Creator of heaven and earth,
    and in Jesus Christ, his only Son, our Lord,

    who was conceived by the Holy Spirit,
    born of the Virgin Mary,
    suffered under Pontius Pilate,
    was crucified, died and was buried;
    he descended into hell;
    on the third day he rose again from the dead;
    he ascended into heaven,
    and is seated at the right hand of God the Father almighty;
    from there he will come to judge the living and the dead.
I believe in the Holy Spirit,
    the holy catholic Church,
    the communion of saints,
    the forgiveness of sins,
    the resurrection of the body,
    and life everlasting. Amen.

Prayer of the Faithful

Reader: *The reader presents our needs to God. We pray silently as the reader prays aloud.*

Reader: We pray to the Lord.
People: Lord, hear our prayer.

Priest: *The priest summarizes our needs. We pray silently as he prays aloud.*
People: Amen.

*In the **Prayer of the Faithful**, we ask God for what we need. We pray for our Church leaders, ourselves, and for others. We pray for all people to live in justice and peace.*

Jesus loves you very much. Trust him. Tell him the concerns that are in your heart. Write or draw them below.

Welcome, Children!

When we gather for celebrations, we often share a meal. This part of Mass is called the **Liturgy of the Eucharist**.

During the **Presentation of the Gifts**, we bring symbols of love to the table of Jesus. These gifts show our gratitude for all God's blessings. God will bless our gifts and give us the greatest gift: Jesus himself in the Holy Eucharist.

Match the gifts on the left side with the gifts on the right.

God's Gifts to Us   **Our Gifts to God**

LITURGY OF THE EUCHARIST

Offertory Song
While the gifts are being brought to the altar, we sing a song.

Presentation of the Gifts

Priest: Blessed are you, Lord God of all creation,
for through your goodness we have received
the bread we offer you:
fruit of the earth and work of human hands,
it will become for us the bread of life.
People: Blessed be God for ever.

Priest: Blessed are you, Lord God of all creation,
for through your goodness we have received
the wine we offer you:
fruit of the vine and work of human hands,
it will become our spiritual drink.
People: Blessed be God for ever.

Invitation to Prayer

Priest: Pray, brethren (brothers and sisters),
that my sacrifice and yours
may be acceptable to God,
the almighty Father.
People: May the Lord accept the sacrifice
at your hands
for the praise and glory of his name,
for our good
and the good of all his holy Church.

Welcome, Children!

Our gifts of bread and wine become the Body and Blood of Christ. This is the Holy Eucharist, or Mass, the special meal that Jesus invites us to attend.

Special dishes are used to serve the meal. Look for them on the altar in your church. Which ones can you name? Lay a pencil along the dotted lines to find out.

This plate holds the bread.

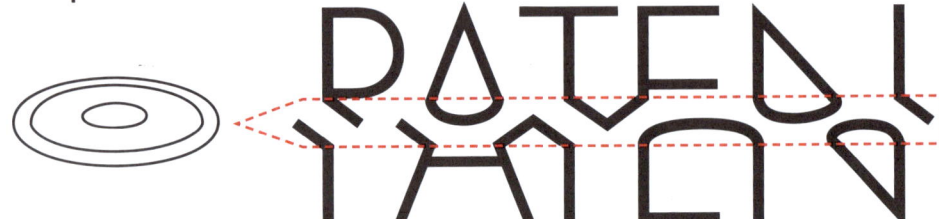

This cup contains the wine.

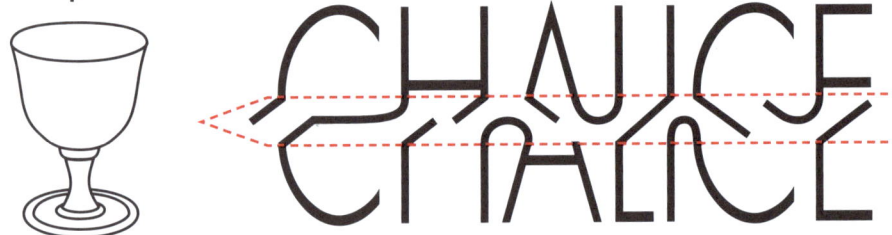

These containers carry the water and wine.

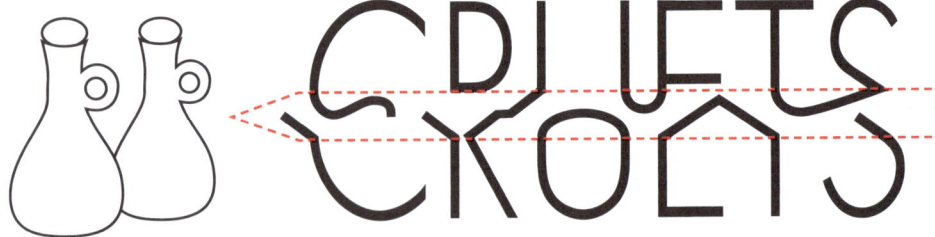

This table represents the table of Jesus.

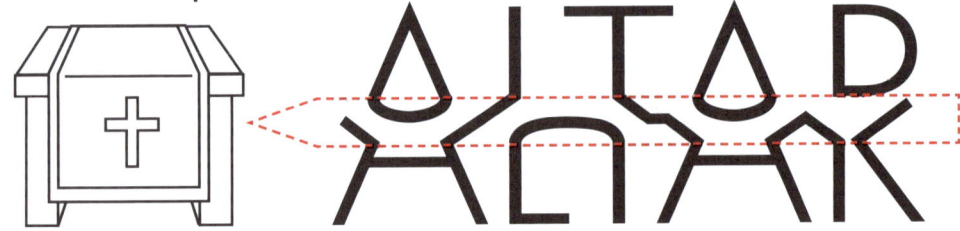

Prayer Over the Gifts

Priest: *The priest asks God to bless and accept our gifts. We pray silently as he prays aloud.*
People: Amen.

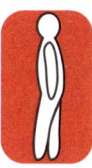

Eucharistic Prayer

Priest: The Lord be with you.
People: And with your spirit.
Priest: Lift up your hearts.
People: We lift them up to the Lord.
Priest: Let us give thanks to the Lord our God.
People: It is right and just.

Priest: *The priest says a prayer of thankfulness and praise. We pray silently as he prays aloud. When he invites us to respond, we say or sing:*

Priest and **People:**

Holy, Holy, Holy Lord God of hosts.
Heaven and earth are full of your glory.
Hosanna in the highest.
Blessed is he who comes in the name of the Lord.
Hosanna in the highest.

Priest: *The priest recalls the story of Jesus' Last Supper. We pray silently as he prays aloud.*

Welcome, Children!

As Jesus' friends, we accept events of his life, even though we don't understand them. These mysteries show us the power of God! In the **Memorial Acclamation**, we show our acceptance. Can you memorize the three responses?

This maze reveals a mystery-message from Jesus. Each single letter is the beginning of a word choice below. Follow the path to find the words. Follow Jesus to find the mystery!

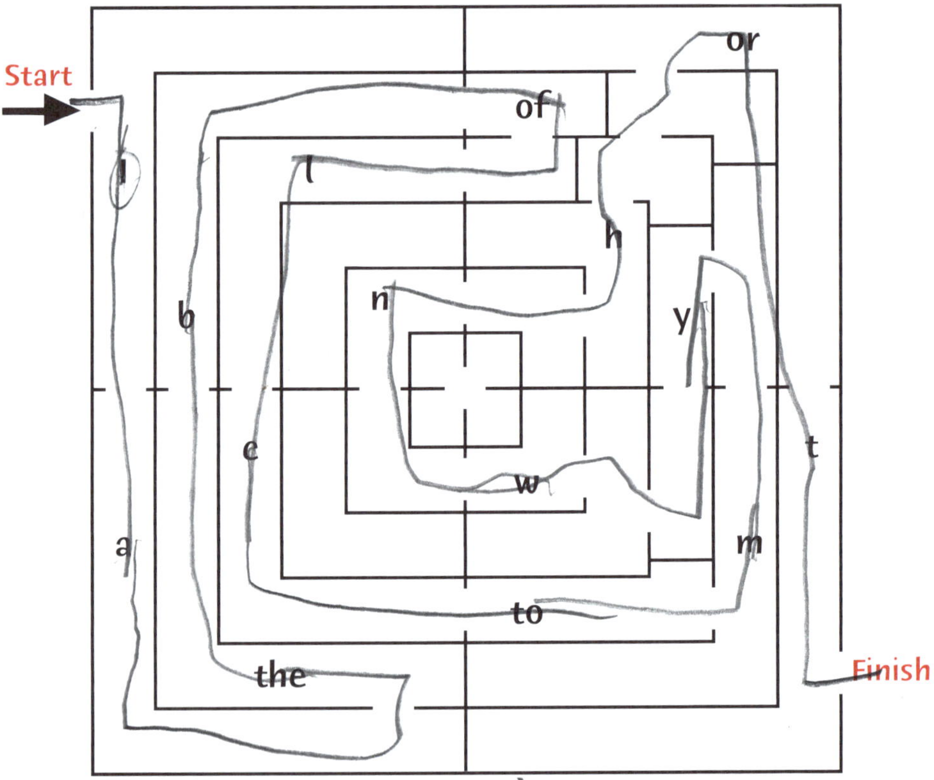

Word choices: am, bread, come, hunger, I, life, me, not, thirst, will, you

The mystery message is in your Bible. Look in John 6:35.

Eucharistic Prayer, continued

The bread and wine are consecrated with these words:
Priest: TAKE THIS, ALL OF YOU, AND EAT OF IT,
FOR THIS IS MY BODY,
WHICH WILL BE GIVEN UP FOR YOU.

Priest: TAKE THIS, ALL OF YOU, AND DRINK FROM IT,
FOR THIS IS THE CHALICE OF MY BLOOD,
THE BLOOD OF THE NEW AND ETERNAL COVENANT,
WHICH WILL BE POURED OUT FOR YOU AND FOR MANY
FOR THE FORGIVENESS OF SINS.
DO THIS IN MEMORY OF ME.

Memorial Acclamation

Priest: The mystery of faith.
People: We proclaim your Death, O Lord,
and profess your Resurrection
until you come again.

[or] When we eat this Bread and drink this Cup,
we proclaim your Death, O Lord,
until you come again.

[or] Save us, Savior of the world,
for by your Cross and Resurrection,
you have set us free.

We continue to pray silently as the priest prays aloud. At the end of the prayer, the priest prays the following words:
Priest: Through him, and with him, and in him,
O God, almighty Father,
in the unity of the Holy Spirit,
all glory and honor is yours,
for ever and ever.
People: Amen.

When we pray **The Lord's Prayer**, we are united with all of Jesus' friends—past, present, and future.

Prayers come from our hearts when we understand them. You don't have to be puzzled! You can learn the big words in this prayer. Underline each word choice in the Lord's Prayer on the next page. Then fill in the puzzle below.

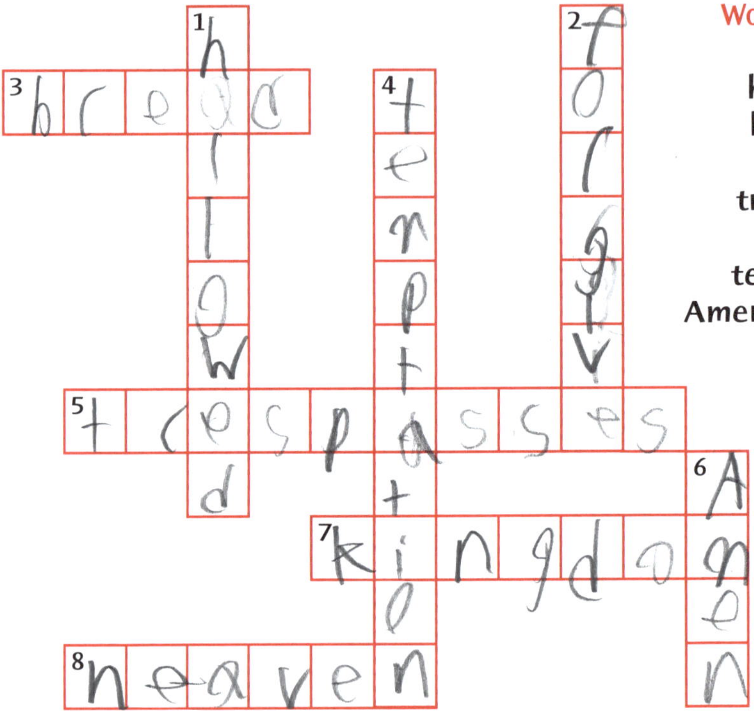

Word choices:
heaven
hallowed
kingdom
bread
trespasses
forgive
temptation
Amen (Bonus Word!)

Across
3 Physical and spiritual food
5 Unloving words and unloving actions
7 A way of life where God reigns and love rules
8 Being in God's presence forever

Down
1 Holy and sacred
2 To show mercy and love
4 Thoughts and things that invite unloving actions
6 Yes, I agree!

24

The Lord's Prayer

Priest: At the Savior's command
and formed by divine teaching,
we dare to say:

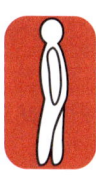

Priest and **People:**

Our Father, who art in heaven,
hallowed be thy name;
thy kingdom come,
thy will be done
on earth as it is in heaven.
Give us this day our daily bread,
and forgive us our trespasses,
as we forgive those who trespass against us;
and lead us not into temptation,
but deliver us from evil.

Priest: Deliver us, Lord, we pray, from every evil,
graciously grant peace in our days,
that, by the help of your mercy,
we may be always free from sin
and safe from all distress,
as we await the blessed hope
and the coming of our Savior, Jesus Christ.

People: For the kingdom, the power, and the glory
are yours, now and for ever.

Many years ago, Jesus' friends asked him how to pray. The story is in your Bible. Look in Luke 11:1-4. What did Jesus say? Compare his words with the Lord's Prayer above.

Sign of Peace

Priest: Lord Jesus Christ,
who said to your Apostles:
Peace I leave you, my peace I give you,
look not on our sins,
but on the faith of your Church,
and graciously grant her peace and unity
in accordance with your will.
Who live and reign for ever and ever.

People: Amen.

Priest: The peace of the Lord be with you always.
People: And with your spirit.
Priest: Let us offer each other the sign of peace.

Shake hands with the people around you and say, "Peace be with you."

During the **Sign of Peace**, we greet one another as Jesus greeted his friends. Jesus wants us to feel his peace, too.

What are some signs of peace in the world? Color these. Create your own. Be a sign of peace to other people!

Breaking of the Bread

People: Lamb of God, you take away the sins of the world, have mercy on us.
Lamb of God, you take away the sins of the world, have mercy on us.
Lamb of God, you take away the sins of the world, grant us peace.

Many years ago, Jesus broke bread and shared it with his friends. The stories are in your Bible. Look in John 6:1-14. Who shared the bread with Jesus? At Mass, Jesus continues to break bread and share it with his friends—us!

At ordinary meals, you can share bread, too. Ask an adult to help with this recipe. When the bread has cooled, say "Thank you" to God. Then share it with everyone at your table. What else can you share?

Homemade Bread

1 pkg. active dry yeast
1/4 cup warm water
1 tsp. sugar
1 cup evaporated milk

1 cup whole wheat flour
1 1/4 cup white flour
1/2 tsp. salt
2 tbsp. plus 2 tsp. sugar

Dissolve yeast in warm water. Add 1 teaspoon sugar. Let stand 5 minutes until foamy. Add milk. In a medium-sized bowl, combine flours, salt, and remaining sugar. Make a well in the center and pour in the yeast mixture. Beat 50 strokes. Turn onto greased baking sheet. Form into 8" circle and let rise 30 minutes in a warm place. Bake at 400 degrees for 20-30 minutes or until golden. Brush top with melted butter. Cool. Break into pieces and serve.

Welcome, Children!

Jesus welcomes everyone to his table!

—To receive a blessing (if you have not received your First Eucharist), hold your arms across your chest when you approach the priest or extraordinary minister of Holy Communion.

—To receive Holy Communion, bow your head to show reverence for the Body and Blood of Christ. Hold out your hands, one hand beneath the other, to receive the host. Or you may open your mouth and extend your tongue to receive the host.

Use both hands to receive the cup.

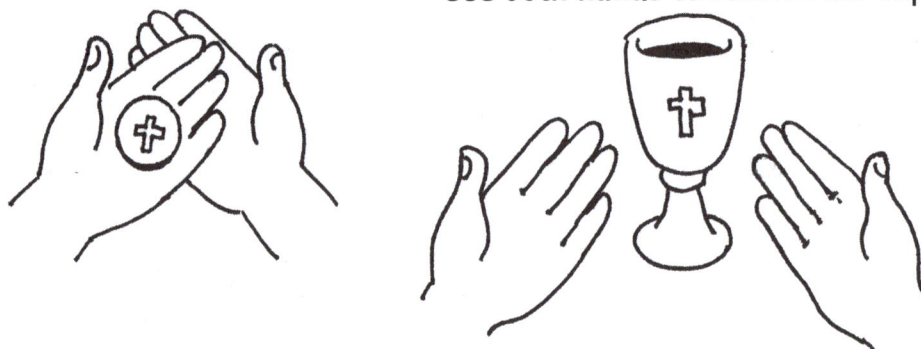

Eucharist means "thanksgiving." When you return to the pew, thank God for all your blessings. Think of a blessing for each letter in your name. Write or draw them across both pages below.

Communion Prayer

Priest: Behold the Lamb of God,
behold him who takes away the sins of the world.
Blessed are those called to the supper of the Lamb.
People: Lord, I am not worthy
that you should enter under my roof,
but only say the word
and my soul shall be healed.

Receiving Communion

After the priest and ministers receive the Body and Blood of Christ, we approach to receive Holy Communion.
Priest or Minister: The Body/Blood of Christ.
Each person: Amen.

Meditation: Silence or Song of Praise

Prayer after Communion

Priest: Let us pray...
The priest prays for all of us to be strengthened by the Eucharist. We pray silently as he prays aloud. At the end of the prayer, we respond:
People: Amen.

CONCLUDING RITE

Priest: The Lord be with you.
People: And with your spirit.

Priest: May almighty God bless you,
the Father,
and the Son,
and the Holy Spirit.
People: Amen.

Priest: Go forth, the Mass is ended.
[or] Go and announce the Gospel of the Lord.
[or] Go in peace, glorifying the Lord by your life.
[or] Go in peace.
People: Thanks be to God.

Closing Song

Mass is over. What begins? Block out the L's and R's in this puzzle. Follow the trail to find the words.

the END of EACH MASS IS THE BEGINNING OF SOMETHING NEW INSIDE OF YOU

Welcome, Children!

Congratulations! You are growing in friendship with Jesus. You have attended his special gathering. You have participated in the Mass. Come back soon!

Write the words "Go in Peace" on top of this door. Color the spaces like a checkerboard. Read the words from the first color. Then read the words from the second color.

WHEN	YOU	YOU	CAN
SHARE	LEAVE,	THIS	YOU
CARRY	LOVE	JESUS'	WITH
THE	LOVE	PEOPLE	IN
YOUR	AROUND	HEART	YOU

Welcome, Children!

Welcome back to daily life! You can share Jesus' love in many ways and in many places. Here are some suggestions, but they are written backwards. Rewrite them on the lines beside each word. Go forward with love!

gnitarepooc _____

_____ gnitcepser

gninetsil _____

gniyalp _____

_____ gnirac

gnirahs _____

_____ gnilims

gnipleh _____

_____ gniyarp

32